THE CALLIGRAPHY SOURCE BOOK

A Book of Lettering

This edition published by Magna Books Ltd,
Magna Road, Wigston, Leicester, LE18 4ZH,
produced by The Promotional Reprint Company Ltd.

Originally produced by A & C Black Ltd., 1926

ISBN 1 85422 446 8

Printed in China

INTRODUCTION

THE letters which we are so accustomed to regard as standing for sounds, and giving us, in combinations, every word we use, had an origin in prehistoric time. Every primitive race had some means of scratching or carving crude pictures to tell a story on the walls of their cave dwelling, on wood, bone, or stone. Certain objects were represented in a definite way, and in the case of the Egyptians the well-known hieroglyphics were evolved.

Gradually the crude pictures became conventionalized and began to stand for words and ideas rather than for objects. It was not a far step from words or syllables to sounds, and this the Phoenicians accomplished by borrowing the cursive or abridged form of the Egyptian hieroglyphic writing, and developing from it the alphabet of sound-symbols which became the mother alphabet of the Greek, the Roman, and eventually of all the modern European alphabets.

The Romans produced an alphabet bold and direct like themselves, and the alphabet on the Trajan column remains as a grand though simple monument to this wonderful nation. The Roman alphabet is given on page 5, and you can see that it is the foundation of every alphabet we use. Its accurate simplicity was eminently suitable for the purpose of carving inscriptions—grand inscriptions—on stone.

It is, of course, inevitable that the tool used for making the letters and the material in which they were made should influence their shape. Manuscripts written with a soft quill or a reed began to exhibit curves and ornaments ; sometimes letters were tied together. By the fifth century a complete alphabet of small letters had been evolved, and by the eighth century capital and small letters were in general use.

Many other nations beside the Romans had begun to have an influence in literature, and therefore on writing, before the tenth century. One of the alphabets that has made a lasting impression because of its great beauty is the Lombardic, still famous for its clearness and artistic excellence.

Roman missionaries took manuscripts into Ireland, and the Irish monks, from the fifth century onwards, developed and preserved a model of lettering which reached the height of perfection in the wonderful Book of Kells. Some examples of the lettering from this source are given here. The arrival of Irish missionaries in England caused the earliest English manuscripts to resemble the Irish, as the writing in the famous Lindisfarne or Durham Book proves.

It was an Englishman, Alcuin of York, who, during the ninth century, as Abbot of Tours, was entrusted by Charlemagne with the work of rewriting all the religious books of the Empire. He introduced changes in the accepted forms which gave not only beautiful, but exceedingly legible, writing. It became so popular that it influenced all the writing in Europe right up to the time when printing was invented. If you look at the Tours manuscripts they remind you, in their clearness, of some of the " print-writing " in our schools to-day.

Naturally this " Caroline " writing (as it was called) did not remain unchanged between the ninth and thirteenth centuries, and one of its descendants—the Gothic—was used widely in England, and indeed is still used for special decorative work. You can find some beautiful Gothic lettering on the tomb of Richard II. in Westminster Abbey (1399).

During this period the letters began to show the thick and thin strokes which we now accept as a matter of course, and initial letters increased in number and design. It was during the Middle Ages that I and U were duplicated into J and V.

It may be as well to remind you here of the kind of material which influenced the details of lettering. For carving on slate (as for tombs) the letters must not have sharp corners or the slate might chip. On brass, such a limitation was not necessary, and so the lettering on brass could be (and was) much more varied in its ornamentation ; so too on stone.

Seals in early days were of great importance, and the craftsman had to consider the letters he would carve, with a view not only to boldness, but also to the fact that they formed a circular, not a straight impression, and had usually to fit in with some heraldic device. The same limitations would apply to medals and coins.

For pottery, or for castings of bells or cannon, a pliable material was used ; the letters modelled on the castings, for instance, would have to be adapted to the behaviour of the molten metal. Wrought iron, again, would be twisted into alpha-betic designs on screens, and the necessary joining of the letters to the rest of the work would cause their decoration to become an essential part of the general design.

In the domestic realm wood was a material treated with loving care, the names of their owners often being carved on beautiful chests or dressers. Among metal utensils decorated by artistic letterings were flagons, dishes, and even warming-pans.

As for manuscripts, charters, and diplomatic writing of all sorts, their number was legion, and their legibility sometimes degenerated either by practice or by design. In these days engrossing is still an art essential in the preparation of legal documents.

It was the fifteenth century that saw the introduction of printing with separate types (or typography), and for centuries afterwards discussion waged as to the rival claims of Coster of Haarlem and Gutenberg of Mainz for the distinction of being its first discoverer. To us it is of more interest to know that William Caxton, while representing the Merchant Adventurers Company in Bruges, learnt the art of printing from Colard Mansion. At Bruges he translated and printed " The Recuyell of the Historyes of Troye," which was thus the first book ever printed in English. He followed it in 1475 by " The Game & Playe of the Chesse," and then returned to England. In 1477 he printed at Westminster " The Dictes & Sayings of the Philosophers," and this was probably the first book ever printed in this country. He continued using his printing press in Westminster—where he was visited by King Edward IV—till his death about 1491. One of the finest collections of the books which he printed is to be found in the John Rylands Library in Manchester.

From this time there have been high and low levels in the art of printing, probably the lowest having been reached about a century ago. Then arose William Caslon, who, beginning as an engraver of gun barrels, gradually turned his attention to type cutting. His type set a new model of clear lettering, and remains in use to-day by those wanting honest and unaffected printing. The leading printers to-day are going back to the beautiful and simple forms of Roman letter employed by the Italian printers of the seventies of the fifteenth century, when printing reached the high-water mark of perfection.

We have endeavoured to give in this book examples of lettering suitable to the needs of different crafts and materials, and have added at the end, examples of printing and type used for different purposes.

L. EDNA WALTER.

June 1926.

PRINT WRITING

Here is a simplified form of lettering based on the Roman (see pages 7 and 9). It is a suitable type for children to use.

ABCDEFGH
IJKLMNOP
QRSTUVW
XYZ. & &

abcdefghijklmno
pqrstuvwxyz.&&

1234567890

ROMAN LETTERING

CAPITALS

This is probably the simplest and most dignified style of lettering produced by any nation. The alphabet is taken from the inscription cut in the stone of the Trajan column in Rome.

It is suitable for most purposes.

ABCDEFG

HIJKLMN

OPQRSTU

VWXYZ&

1234567

890O6&&

ROMAN LETTERING

SMALL LETTERS

These are essentially letters to be written with a pen or quill.

If a flowing hand is desired the letters should be tied at the bottom wherever possible.

a b c d e f g h i j

k l m n o p q r s

t u v w x y z or ʒ

a b c d e f g h i j k l

m n o p q r s t u v

w x y z or ʒ . & Ↄ Ɛ

1 2 3 4 5 6 7 8 9 0

ROMAN LETTERING

CAPITALS DRAWN WITH A SLANTED NIB

This alphabet of capitals, made by using a broad slanted nib, is suitable for initial words or sometimes for whole pages of special printing where dignity is desired, such as for prayers or altar books.

ABCDEFG

HIJKLMN

OPQRST

UVWXYZ

1234567

890.&G&

ROMAN LETTERING

SMALL LETTERS DRAWN WITH A SLANTED NIB

This corresponds with the capitals on the previous page and is used for similar purposes.

a b c d e f g h i j

k l m n o p q r s

t u v w x y z or ʒ

a b c d e f g h i j k l

m n o p q r s t u v

w x y z or ʒ . & & ᵹ

1 2 3 4 5 6 7 8 9 0

CASLON CAPITALS AND
SMALL LETTERS

These simple and unaffected alphabets are an example of Caslon's type and are suitable for every-day use.

ABCDEFGH

IJKLMNOP

QRSTUVW

XYZ.&&&

abcdefghijklmno

pqrstuvwxyz.&&

1234567890

CASLON ITALIC CAPITALS AND SMALL LETTERS

These Caslon Italics are suitable for notices in combination with the alphabets on the preceding page, when certain statements need emphasis.

ABCDEFGH

IJKLMNOP

QRSTUVW

XYZ. & & &

abcdefghijklmno

pqrstuvwxyz.& &

1234567890

DECORATIVE PRINTING

This alphabet is suitable for posters, show-cards or notices.

ABCDEFG
hIjKLmN
OpqRST
UVWXYZ
1234567
890. &GƷ

GOTHIC CAPITALS

FOR ILLUMINATING, DECORATIVE PRINTING,
CARVING, EMBROIDERY, ETC.

This is modern Black-letter type. It is a picturesque style of lettering suitable for ornamental purposes such as illuminating, carving on furniture, embroidery, etc.

When letters of this type are used for white embroidery a padding should first be made of running stitches, or of satin stitches which slope in a direction different from that of the top stitching.

ABCDEFG

HIJKLMN

OPQRST

UVWXYZ

1234567

890. &&&

GOTHIC SMALL LETTERS

FOR ILLUMINATING, DECORATIVE PRINTING,
CARVING, EMBROIDERY, ETC.

This small Black-letter type is to be used in conjunction with the Capitals on the previous page.

abcdefghij

klmnopqrs

tuvwxyz

1234567 8

90. G&G

Laudamus te

LOMBARDIC CAPITALS

FOR EMBROIDERY, APPLIQUÉ, ETC.

These Lombardic Capitals have been generally used in illuminated manuscripts and are eminently suitable for that purpose. They can also be used very effectively for leather work and, if slightly simplified, for appliqué.

ABCDEFG

HIJRLON

OPQRST

UVWXYZ

1234567

890.&&G

LETTERS AND MONOGRAMS

FOR APPLIQUÉ, CUT-LINEN, OR LEATHER WORK

The first example is for bold appliqué or for leather work. The centre one (*A. V.*) is specially designed for cut-linen (Richelieu) work, when the border and letters are edged both sides with blanket stitch and are linked together by button-hole bars, the background being afterwards cut away. This will be quite nice for leather work if the background is punched.

The bottom monogram (*A.R.*) is similarly treated but has no border.

LETTERS AND MONOGRAMS

FOR WHITE WORK AND DECORATED BACKGROUNDS

The three mongrams at the top of the page are designed for marking on linen. The *B* is worked entirely in satin stitch padded as described on p. 20. The *R* of the *C.R.S.* is similarly worked, but the *C* and *S* are outlined by means of satin stitch worked over a single padding thread; the detail can be worked in seeding. The *T* can be worked in satin stitch and detail left plain.

The letter *M* can be worked either in appliqué on a patterned material or—for Church work—couched solidly in gold, with a worked background pattern in fine coloured silks.

The *M* of the *M.O.* may be worked solidly in satin stitch. The *O* has a raised outline and is filled with seeding.

The letter *G* and the surrounding border may be outlined, and the background threads drawn together with a drawn ground stitch. This method of treating the background is stronger than drawn thread work as no threads are actually cut or removed. It will be necessary to use a somewhat loosely woven linen on which the threads can easily be counted.

The *R* may be treated similarly to the *C* and *S* of the monogram *C.R.S.* in the top line.

The border and the letters *G* and *B* in the following monogram are worked in satin stitch. The *H* has a raised outline and the detail worked in satin stitch.

The *T.S.* and the frame are worked entirely in padded satin stitch

DECORATIVE ALPHABET AND LETTERS FOR NEEDLEPOINT LACE

The first is an Italian decorative alphabet and can be worked by means of appliqué. The solid portions of the letters may be applied to a background of a contrasting colour and stitched down by means of a couched gold thread which, being continued, forms the decorative interlacing.

The second is a lace-maker's alphabet.

It is adapted from a late sixteenth century pattern book in the Victoria and Albert Museum. The letters may be worked in a needlepoint lace stitch consisting of rows of blanket stitches, each fresh row of stitching being worked into the heading of the last. Threads of linen are left to form the squared background. These are afterwards darned over and the other threads of the back are cut away. The small devices are worked in blanket or overcast stitches.

A similar alphabet worked on a linen sampler can be seen in the Textile Department of the same Museum.

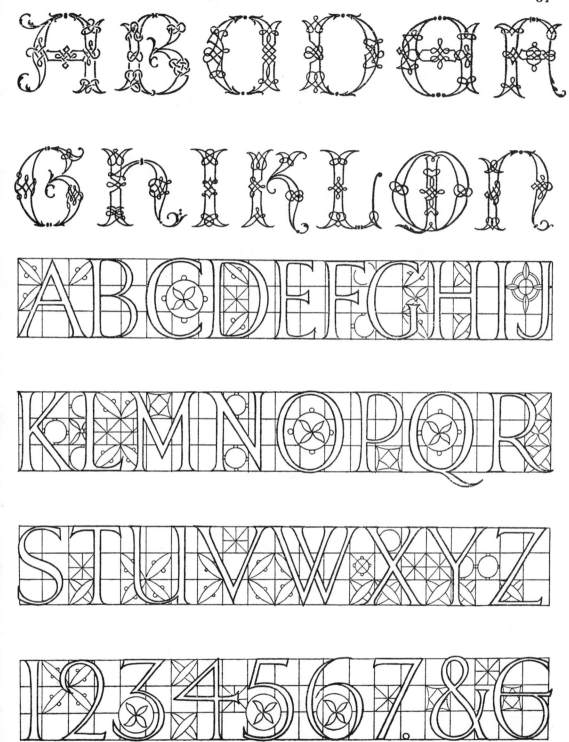

ALPHABET CROSS STITCH

This is a simple alphabet for marking purposes. It may be worked on a loosely woven material on which the threads may be counted. If, however, it is impossible to count the threads, pieces of canvas may be tacked on the fabric, over which the crosses can be made, the canvas threads being afterwards withdrawn.

If the canvas process is adopted the stitches should be tightly worked, or they will appear loose when the canvas is removed.

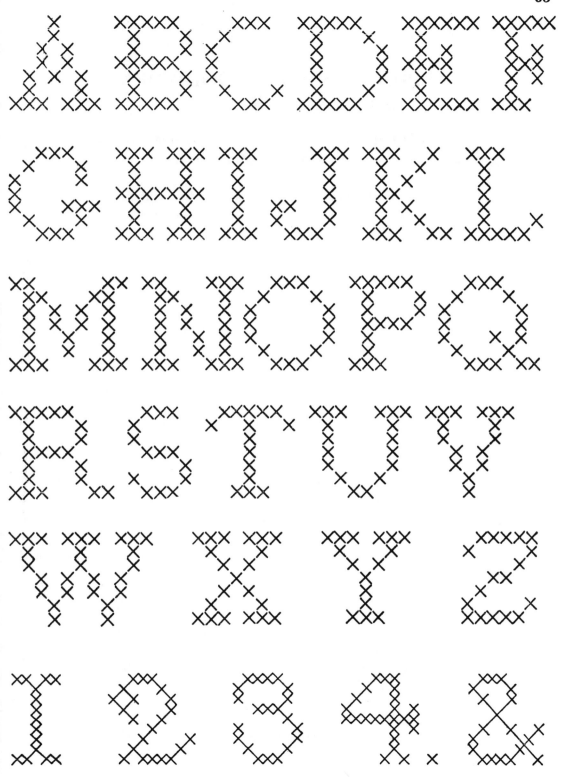

ALPHABETS FOR WOODWORK
OR LEATHER WORK

The first alphabet consists of a very simple form of lettering for woodwork or for leather work, the letters being in relief.

The second, meant to suggest twisted ribbon or thongs of leather, is also suitable for leather work—the shaded parts being well pressed down.

ABCDEFGHIJ
KLMNOPQR
STUVWXYZ

abcdefghij
klmnopqr
stuvwxy3

ALPHABETS FOR REPOUSSÉ, WOODWORK, LEATHER WORK, ETC.

The first alphabet may be used for repoussé work, the letters being in relief on a hammered ground. It may also be used for leather work or woodwork where a similar effect is desired.

The letters below are suitable for woodwork, the darkened portions being gouged out from the relief letters. They can also be used for leather work, when a small punch should press down the darkened details.

ABCDEF
GHIJKLM

ABCDEF
GHIJKLM
123456
7890.&

SINGLE ORNAMENTAL CAPITALS

FOR WOODWORK, REPOUSSÉ, LEATHER, APPLIQUÉ, ETC.

Each of these letters can be treated in one of the different methods described on pages, 27, 29, 37, etc.

LETTERING FOR STENCILLING AND ENGRAVING ON METAL

The first is a simple alphabet designed for stencilling, the letters being cut out in drawing or stencil paper. The colour is then "dabbed" on (not painted), by means of a special stencil brush. Oil paint, or a special stencil paint which will not run, should be used.

The second alphabet is designed for engraving on metal.

A B C D E F

G H I J K L M

A B C D E F

G H I J K L M

1 2 3 4 5 6

7 8 9 0 . &

EXAMPLES OF CELTIC DECORATED LETTERS

SUITABLE FOR ILLUMINATING, LEATHER WORK, BRAIDING, OR ANY ADVANCED WORK TO WHICH THE DIRECTIONS ON PREVIOUS PAGES CAN BE APPLIED.

A.E.R.U. and *V.* are suitable for leather work, and would look particularly well if used in conjunction with interlacing borders. They may be worked entirely in relief or with a punched background. *A*, being bold and simple, would also be useful for woodwork.

D would be an excellent letter to use for braiding—the two continuous interlacing lines being carried out by means of a coloured silk braid, either couched, or stitched with a self-coloured silk.

K would be suitable for needlework and could be worked in appliqué with a couched silk outline in a contrasting colour, the darkened portions being stitched in the same colour as the couching.

L has been taken from a seventh-century manuscript, and could be used for the same purposes as *P* and *S*.

P and *S*, which have been taken from the Book of Kells, were originally illuminated, and are particularly suitable for this purpose. They could also be used with good effect for embroidery, where a single decorated initial is required.

O would look well as an outstanding initial printed by hand.

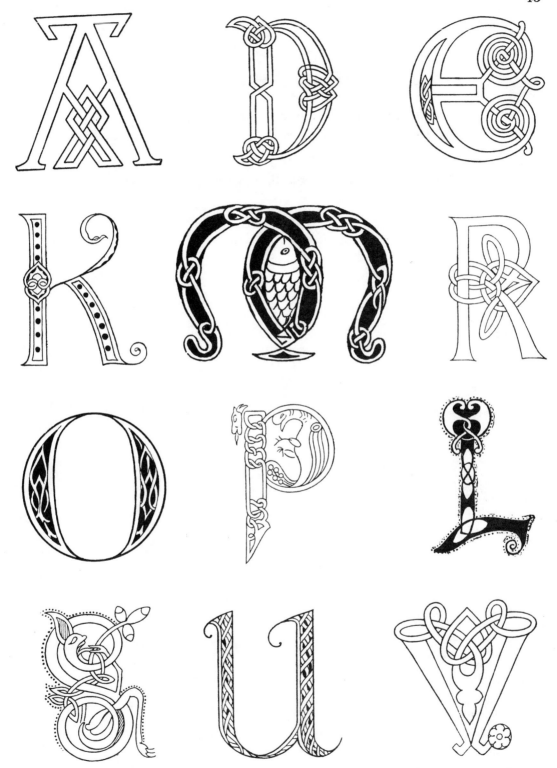

FLOURISHED ITALIC CAPITALS

This alphabet of " swash " capitals is a development of work done in Italy in the sixteenth and seventeenth centuries. Suited best to the pen, it may be used wherever a writing effect, flowing and ornamental, is desired.

A B C D E F

G H I J K L M

N O P Q R S T

U V W X Y Z

1 2 3 4 5 6 7

8 9 0 . & & 6

APPLIED LETTERING
AND DESIGN

These miniature reproductions of book-covers and title-pages are from actual designs by good artists, and are printed here for the guidance of students.

They show the amount of border that can be carried, the balance of the lettering, and some suggestions for decoration.

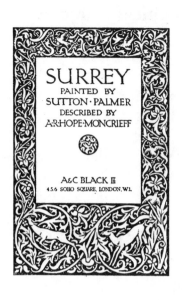

SURREY

PAINTED BY
SUTTON·PALMER
DESCRIBED BY
A·R·HOPE·MONCRIEFF

A&C BLACK L⁰
4.5.6 SOHO SQUARE, LONDON, W.1.

Reduced facsimile of a title-page design

SUPPRESSED
PLATES

G·S·LAYARD

Reduced facsimile of a design on the cloth cover of a book

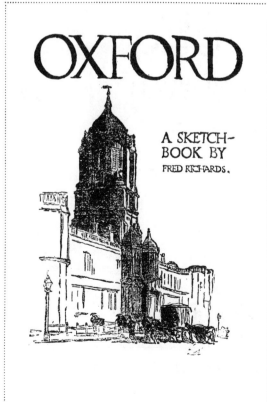

OXFORD

A SKETCH-
BOOK BY
FRED RICHARDS.

Reprint of an actual label used on a book cover

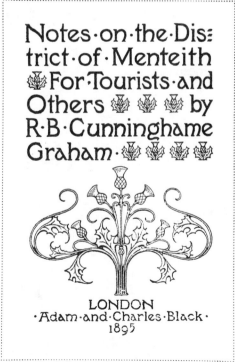

Notes·on·the·Dis=
trict·of·Menteith
For·Tourists·and
Others by
R·B·Cunninghame
Graham·

LONDON
·Adam·and·Charles·Black·
1895

Reduced facsimile of a design on the paper cover of a book

Suggested Headings for Typical Subjects
studied during a week at School.

GARDENING
PLANTING POTATOES

MONDAY   APRIL 24

NEEDLEWORK NOTES
SMOCKING

TUESDAY   APRIL 25

Geography
Regional Survey

Wednesday   April 26

ARITHMETIC
Decimals

Thursday   April 27

HISTORY
MAGNA CARTA

FRIDAY   APRIL 28